The Las

Contents	Page
Goal	2-3
Top secret	4-5
Planning ahead	6-7
Depot-laying	8-11
Different approaches	12-13
Route south	14-15
Weather	16-17
Results	18-19
Victory	20-21
Heroes	22-23
Index	24

written by Rachel Walker

Goal of the Pole

In 1911, the South Pole was one of the last unexplored places on Earth. Captain Robert Scott planned to claim the bottom of the world for the British Empire, while Roald Amundsen hoped to be the first man to reach the South Pole and claim it for his homeland, Norway. It was the "Heroic Age of Antarctic Exploration" – while both expedition parties were determined to succeed, there would be only one winner.

Top secret

Although originally planning to be the first person to reach the North Pole, Amundsen changed his plans and secretly headed South when he learned that two Americans, Robert Peary and Frederick Cook, had already claimed that feat. Amundsen kept his plans for a South Pole expedition to himself, and it wasn't until his ship, "Fram", was well off the coast of Morocco that he even announced to his crew that they were headed for the South, not the North, Pole.

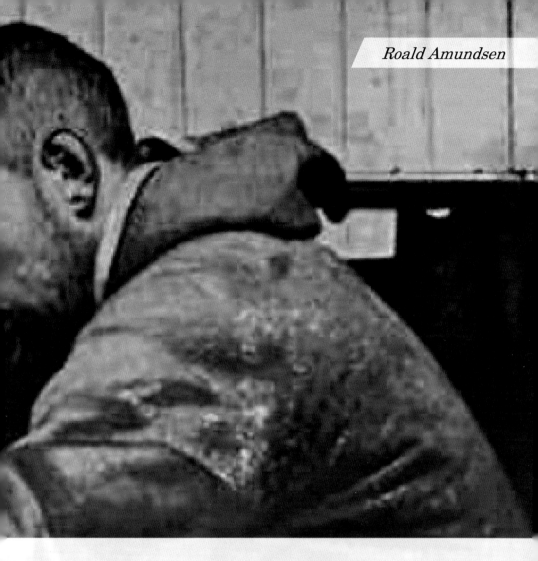

Roald Amundsen

Roald Amundsen was fully aware that Captain Scott was planning the Terra Nova expedition, and he knew many of the details of Scott's plan.

Captain Scott was utterly shocked when he heard about Amundsen's Fram expedition, which had been carefully planned in secret. Suddenly the race to claim the South Pole was on!

Planning ahead

Both the Fram and the Terra Nova expeditions were planned in great detail. Amundsen had spent time learning the survival ways of the Netsilik Inuit people of the North Arctic, while Captain Scott was an experienced explorer too, and had even attempted to reach the South Pole once before. He studied the diaries of Ernest Shackleton from his failed Nimrod expedition 2 years earlier, which came close to, but didn't quite reach, the southernmost point on Earth, failing about 100 miles/160 kms short.

Captain Robert Scott

Depot-laying march

A 1500 mile/2414 km journey on sledges through some of the harshest conditions on Earth takes months to complete, so before the actual expeditions could begin, supply depots had to be set up along the way, with all of the equipment, fuel and food needed for a return trip. Roald Amundsen's supply depot plan took a year to create, with each of the depots being well-stocked:
- plenty of food
- medical supplies
- more than enough fuel for heating and cooking.

Amundsen's sled

Amundsen's depots were well-marked – each with 10 numbered flags carefully spaced at regular intervals on both sides of his depots, so they could be easily found in a blizzard or fog.

Captain Scott's depot-laying plan was quickly formed. He based all his preparations on his previous experience in Antarctica and on notes he had from Shackleton's Nimrod expedition. He didn't really plan for the worst – instead of being well-stocked, each depot contained only enough food and fuel rations for the planned stop, without extra allowance for any bad weather delays or any rest days. There was just one marker flag per depot. Due to bad weather, the last depot was placed 36 miles/60 kms from where it should have been.

supply depot

Different approaches

Amundsen's Fram expedition was simple, as it had only one goal: to reach the Pole first. He took a small team of 5 men with skis and 52 husky dogs to pull sleds.

Scott's Terra Nova expedition also aimed to reach the Pole first, but it had an additional time-consuming purpose: to undertake scientific research along the way. His team started with 16 men, 3 motor sledges and 10 ponies, as well as 23 dogs, and sleds that could be hauled by the men on skis.

Route South

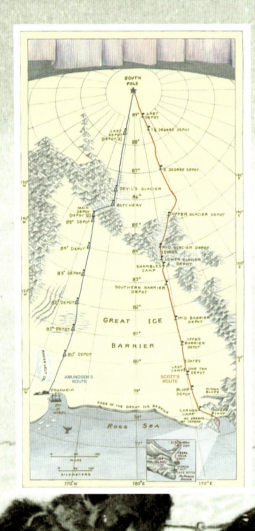

Amundsen set off first, departing in secret on 19th October, 1911. Using skis and teams of dogs pulling sleds, he took a direct route that had never been tried before, starting 60miles/95 kms closer to the Pole from his base camp at the Bay of Whales. It was the straightest path to the Pole; Amundsen was risking unknown terrain, but he was prepared to pioneer the route and go up and over any mountains he found in his path. Five days later, on 24th October, 1911, Captain Scott and his team set off from their base camp at Cape Evans. Leaving from McMurdo Sound, 500 miles/804 kms to the east of Amundsen's base camp at the Bay of Whales, Scott followed the route of Shackleton's failed Nimrod expedition.

Weather

Being 500 miles/804 kms and many days apart, the two expeditions experienced weather conditions that couldn't have been more different. Amundsen's Fram expedition met settled weather and made good progress using their dog-drawn sleds.

Meanwhile Scott's team moved slowly, facing freezing temperatures and blinding white-out blizzards. The motor sledges constantly broke down and had to be abandoned. The ponies could haul heavier sleds than the dogs could, but weren't hardy enough for the harsh, freezing Arctic conditions: sadly none survived the journey. Although the husky dog teams worked well, Captain Scott sent them back to the base camp when they reached the half-way point, because he thought they would struggle in the rougher terrain ahead.

Results

The final stage was undertaken by four men and Captain Scott. The slow and exhausting work of man-hauling the sleds through the snow and ice began. Despite being exhausted, Scott and his men had no choice but to push on through the bone-chilling blizzards from one supply depot to the next. To stay put and rest would have meant certain starvation and death.

Terra Nova team

After 85 gruelling days Captain Scott's Terra Nova expedition successfully reached the South Pole.
To their utter dismay, they found that Amundsen's Fram expedition had beaten them by more than a month, having arrived at the South Pole on the 14th of December, 1911 – a 56-day journey!

Return victory

Having won the race to the South Pole by 29 days, Amundsen and his strong team proudly raised the Norwegian flag, and left a letter claiming the South Pole for their King. Delighted, they started the long return journey to Framheim, arriving safely on 26th January, 1912, taking 99 days to travel the 683 miles/1093 kms round trip. The Norwegians had won the race!

Norwegian flag

Heroes

Bitterly disappointed not to have won, hungry and exhausted, Captain Scott and his team turned to begin the challenging journey back to base camp. The five brave explorers endured frostbite and snow blindness as they experienced fierce blizzards and extreme cold, falling on broken ice and stumbling into crevasses.

Tragically, Captain Scott and his Terra Nova team did not survive the fateful return trip. Starving, weak, and just 11 miles/18 kms short of the relief of their last food depot, Captain Scott wrote his final diary entry:

"Had we lived, I should have had a tale to tell of the hardihood, endurance and courage of my companions which would have stirred the heart of every Englishman."
Captain Scott's Message to the Public, 29th March, 1912.

Index	**Page**
blizzards	17-18, 22
depots	8-10, 18, 23
diaries	6, 23
flags	9-10, 20
husky dogs	12-13, 15, 16-17
motor sledges	13, 17
planning	3-6
ponies	13, 17
scientific research	13
sleds	12, 15